Taking Off The Shoes

By

Natascia Di Terlizzi

Find more about me and my photos
at www.natasciaditerlizzi.com

Self published

Preface

This photopoetry book is a composition made to inspire, sharing parts of my diary, being able to give images to my thoughts and at the same time voice to my photos.

I wrote this diary between two different solo trips that changed my life; the one through England, Scotland and Ireland, that was just finished, and the one through South America, that still had to begin.

During this "break" I found again connection with Mother Nature coming back to the place I grew up: I fed myself with more and more dreams, joy of life, desire to discover and get to know this world; that gave me the strength to go and do everything by myself.

Most of the photos were taken in Prato Drava, a little village in Italy at the border with Austria, where I grew up.

Natascia Di Terlizzi
October 2015

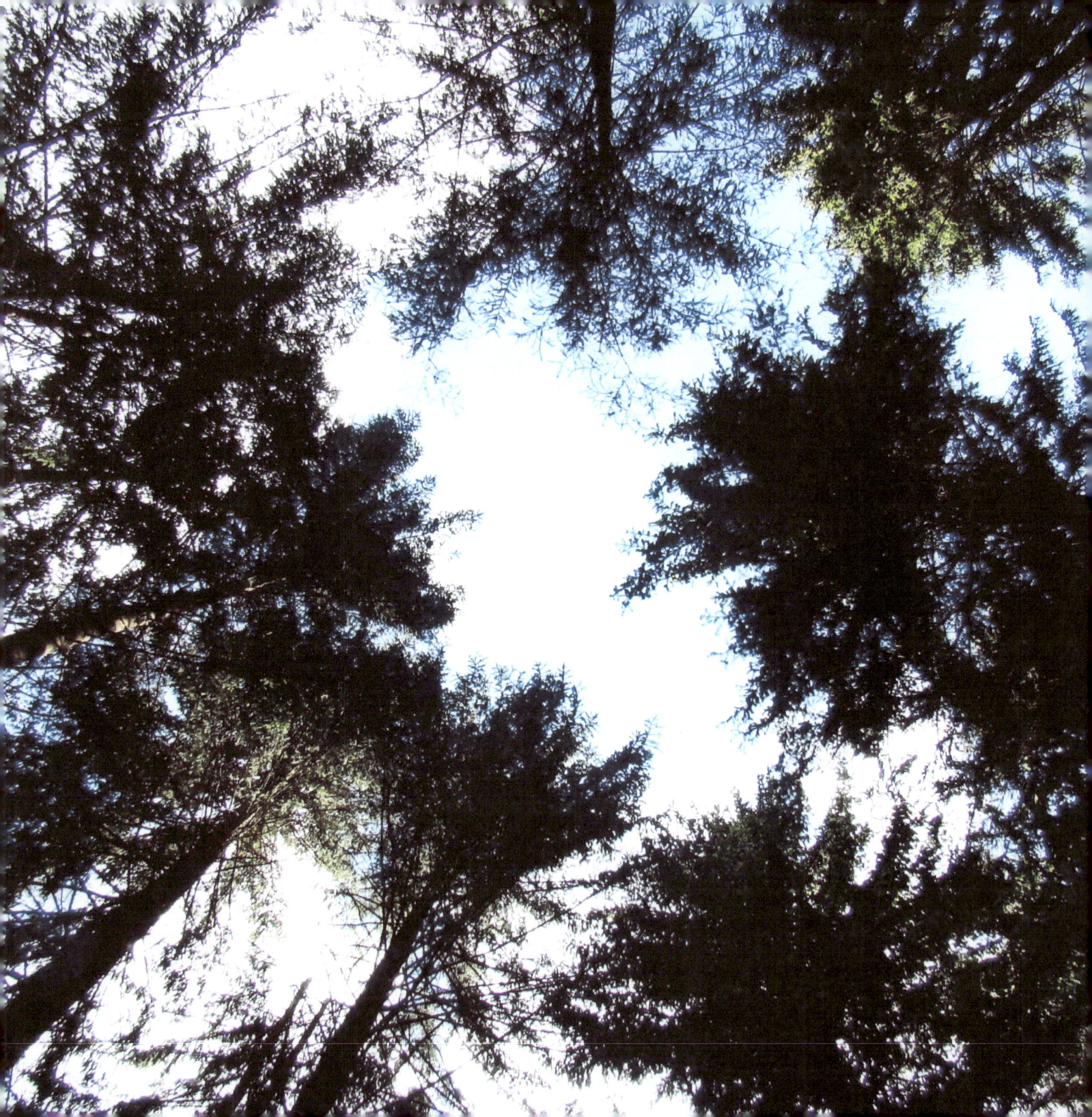

The green arms
Of this branches and leaves,
Include and embrace everything,
Everything sprouts again, grows and
Blooms,
Everything shines back in colour,
In life, in perfume.

And I feel my heart,
In the sun,
That stays still.
Finally all the sighs lay in a tomb
Of a far away cemetry.

Now the eyes caress
The clouds
With a finger,
They sketch houses between the stars
In the infinite sky.

I am leaving on this piece of paper
Simple words,
And who knows if ever readen
By someone else
They will take a new flavour.

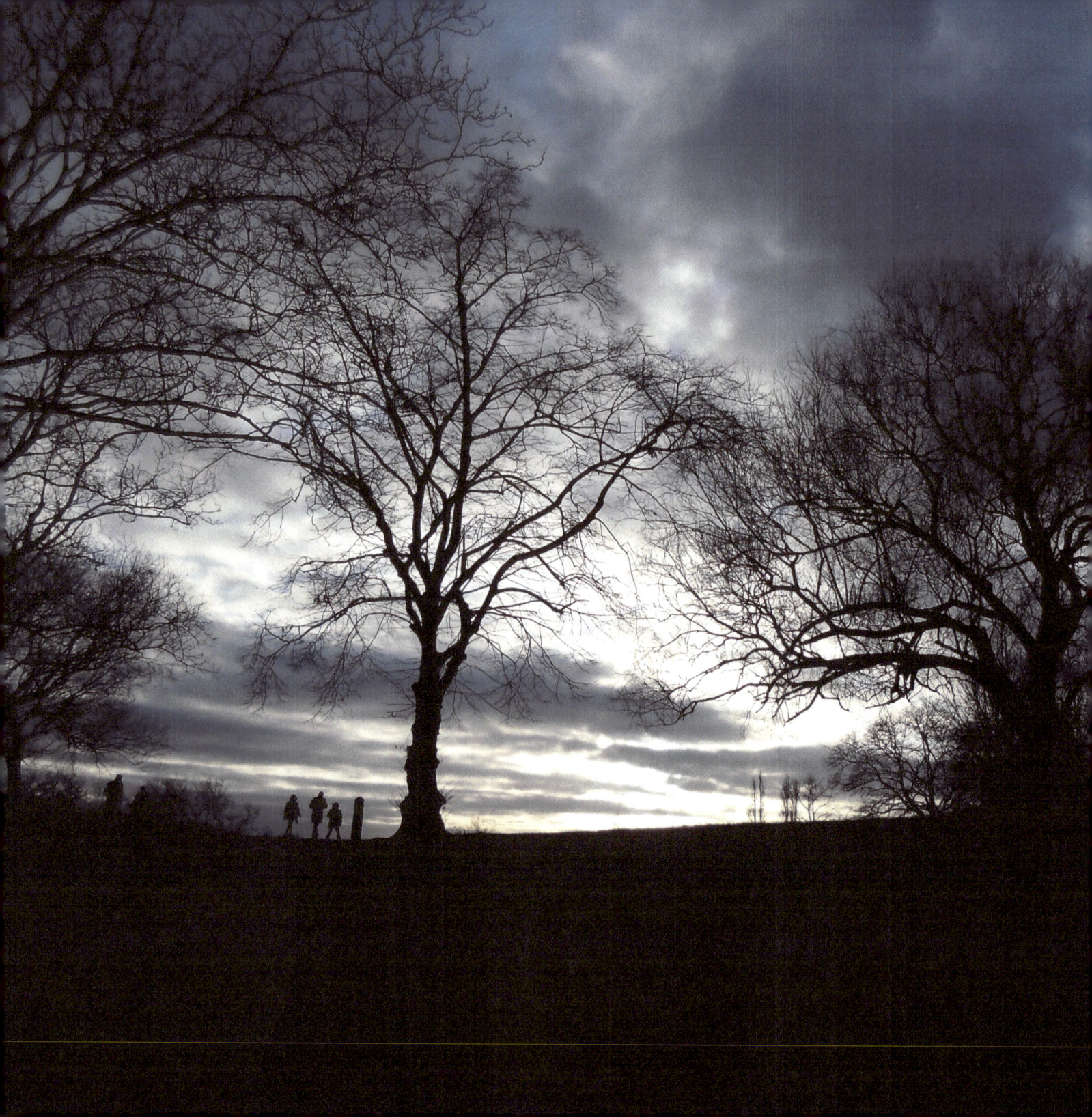

Stuck in the clouds
With the view over the world,
Only a little slice of earth.
Lulled by the notes of this song.

Barefoot through the world
I melt with the Earth,
I want to see and discover,
Open every door,
I want to try every taste,
Breath sea breeze,
Close my eyes and dream,
Smell every perfume.
I want to live this life
With all its ups and downs.

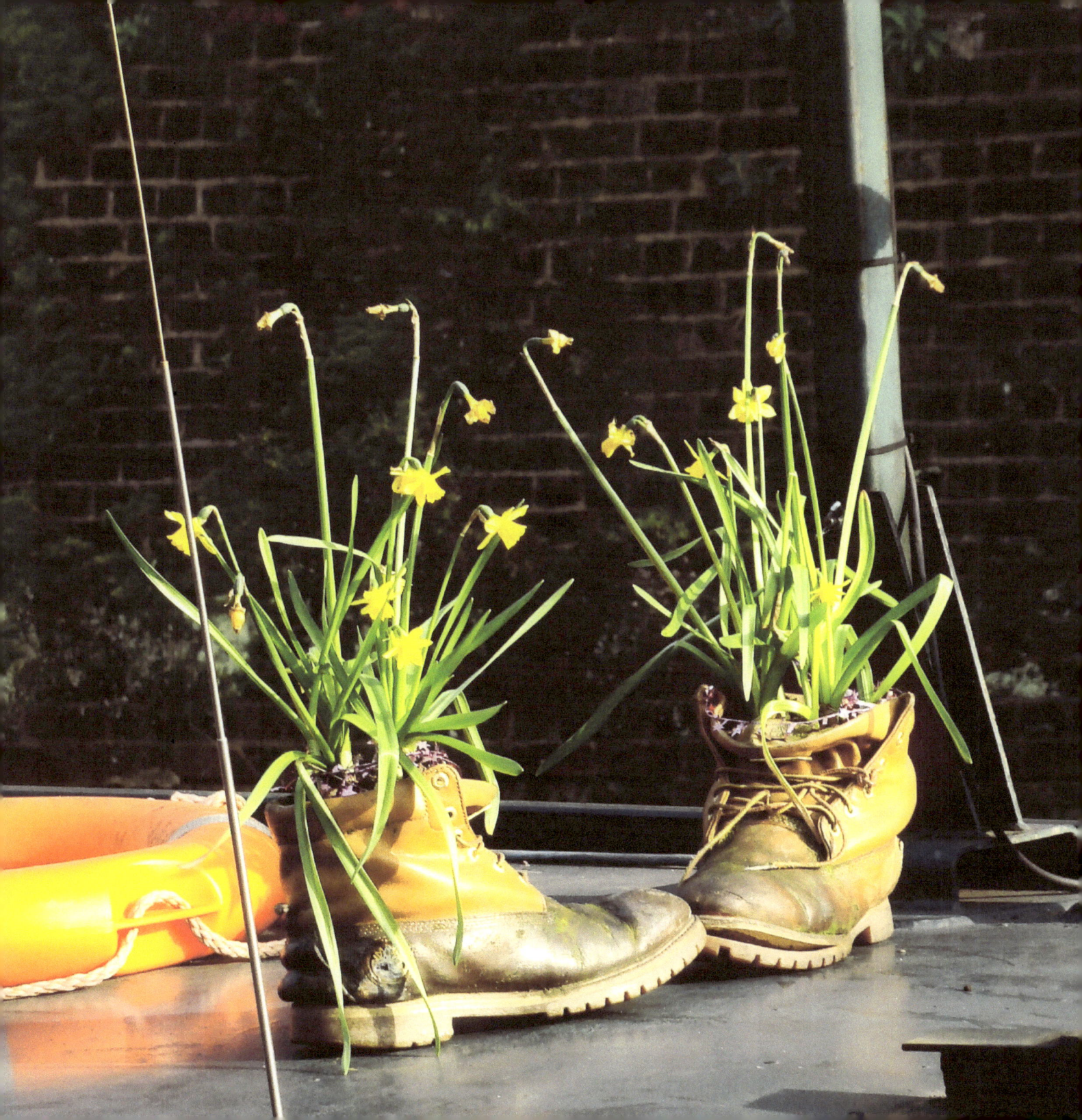

The ink of this journey
To the wise old men tells a little only
Who's lived already in lots of places,
Attended a lot of sunrises.
I can't feel my heart beat anymore,
I think I have to go away
Somewhere
Anyway.

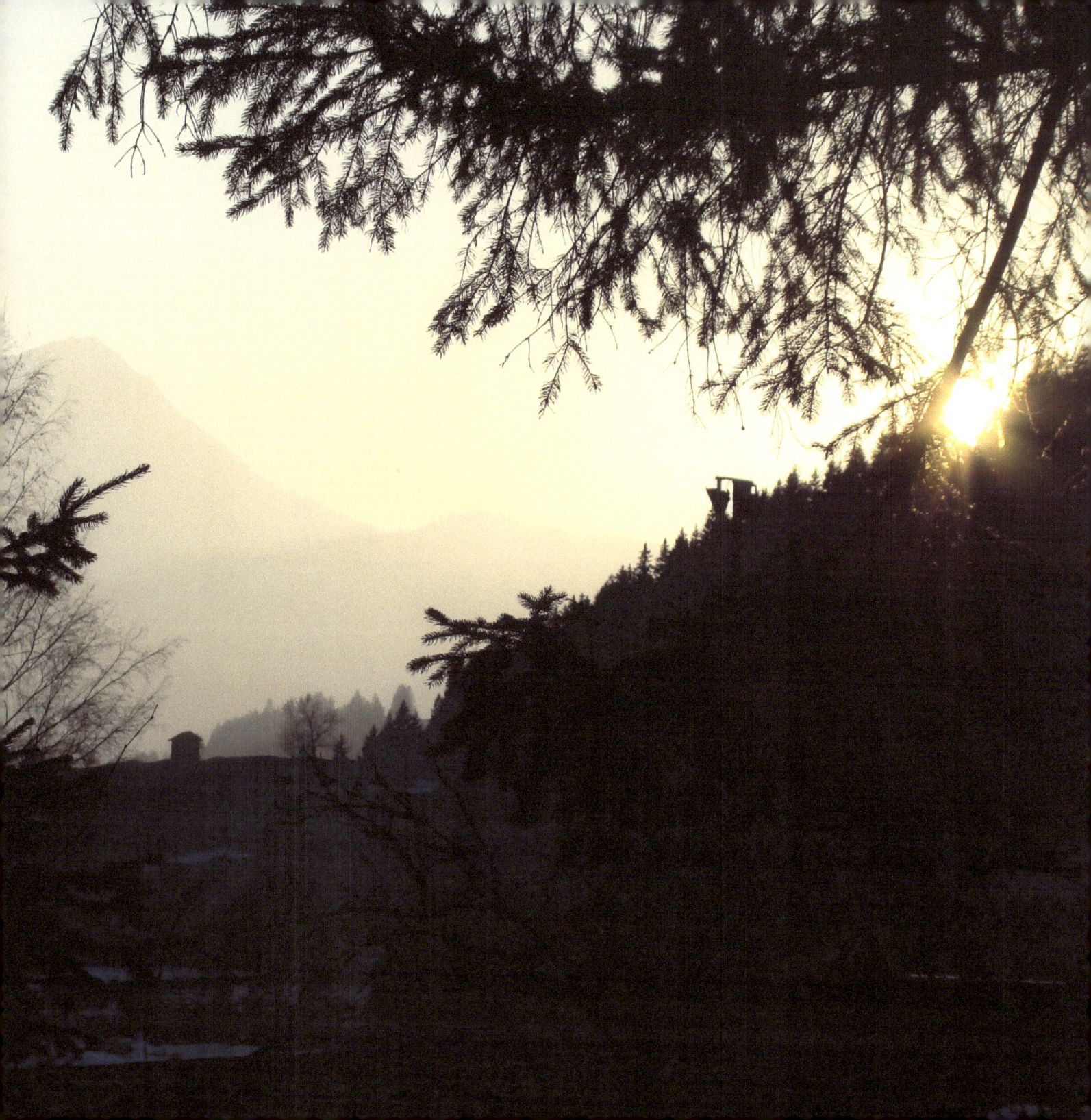

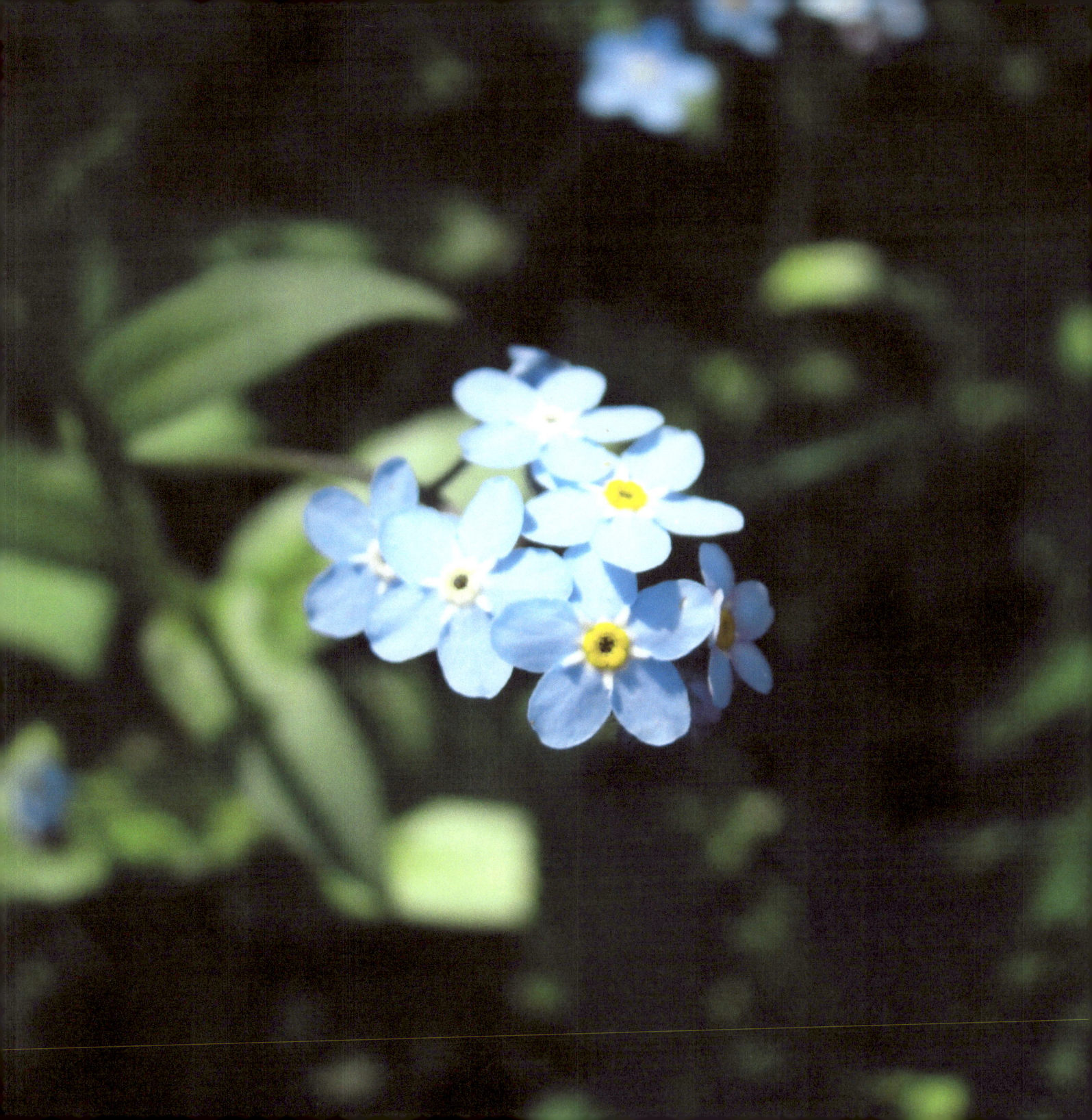

So many words in my head,
So many scars in my heart,
So many cuts on my hands,
So much blood on my fingers.
You leave and you go,
No one follows,
You sing and you dance,
You cry, but
The sky is full of stars
And the field full of flowers.
Through the tears your eyes
Shine, you can see clearer
Afterwards; you look pretty
when you smile, everything
is gonna be fine.

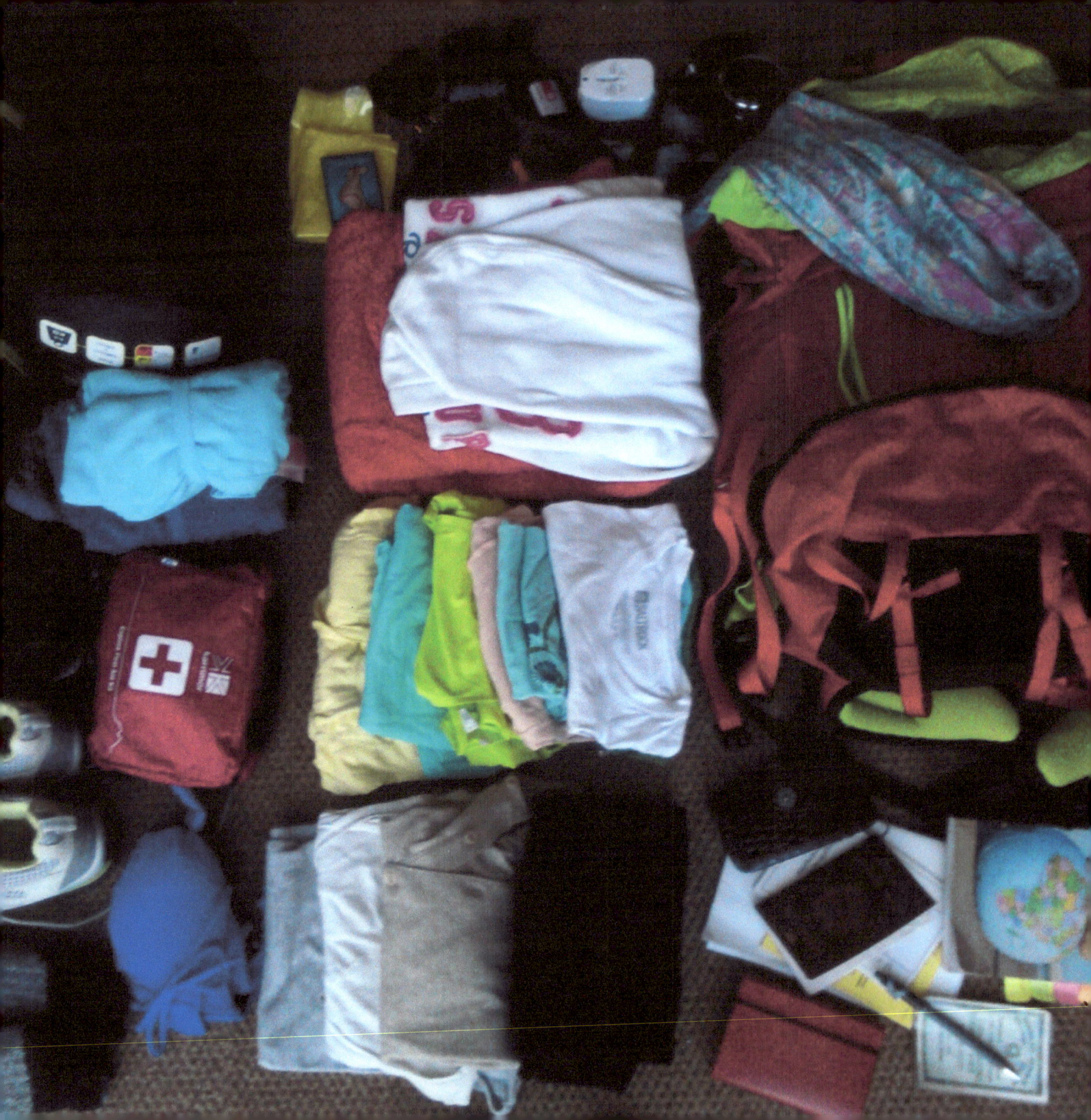

Take your rucksack
And never look back,
There is a world waiting
For you out there,
Not for your tears,
Not for your fears,
But for your smile,
Because it makes you and
What's around you
Shine.
Beautiful soul,
Follow your dreams.

Alone

But never lonely.

How can the river be so constant with its flow?
How can everything become green again
After such a cold winter?
How can the sun be warm again?

Sitting comfortably here
Surrounded by trees,
By that perfume that reminds me
Fresh summer and
Strawberries.
Nature is so calm and
Peaceful.

There is no better therapy
Than sitting in silence with
The nature and just listen
To the songs of the birds,
The speech of the river,
The stories of the wind.

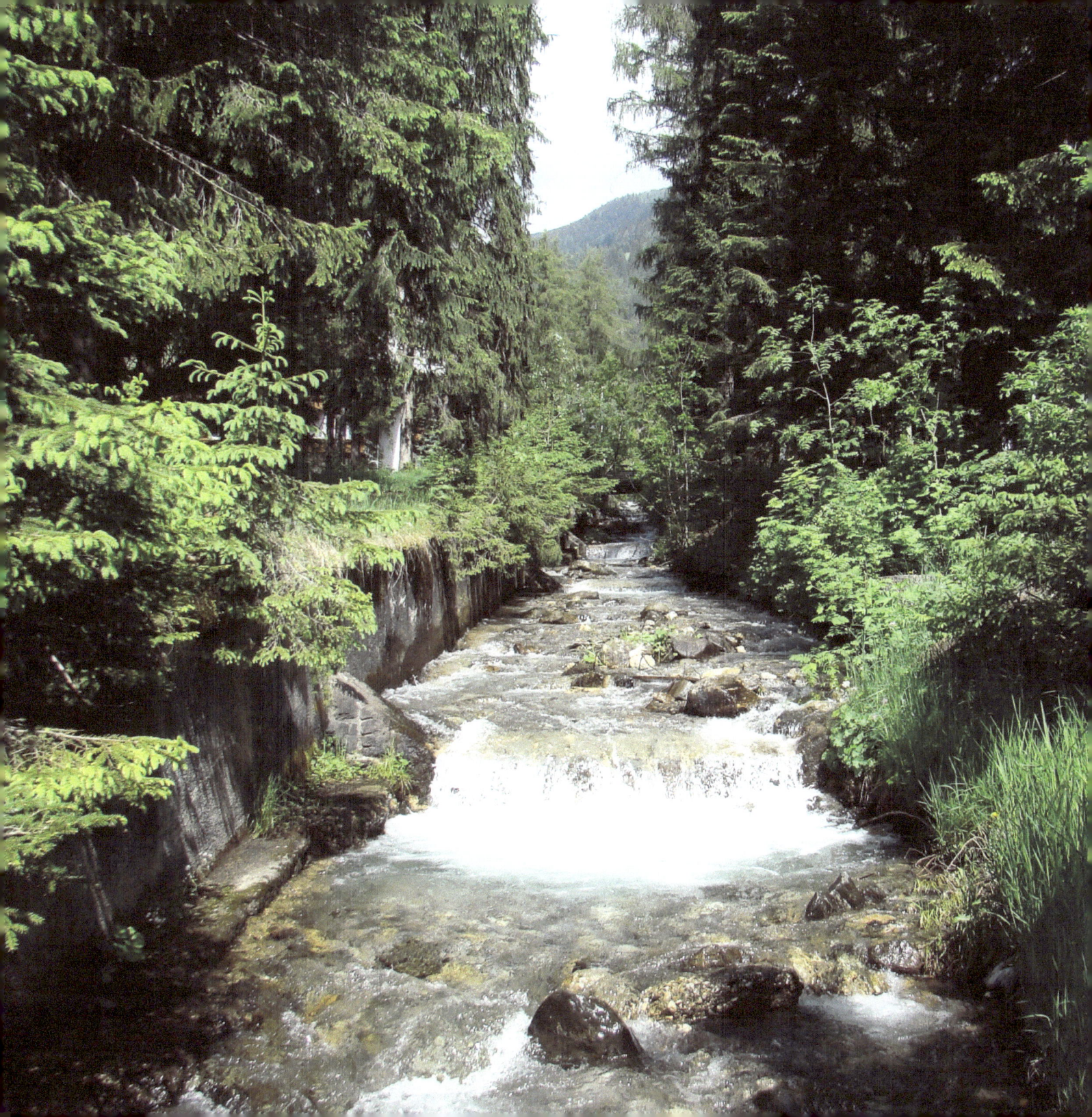

Crying in front of the
Mirror
I see the trails of
My tears designed slowly
On my cheeks.
A salty water drop
That ends
On my lips and
Reminds me
The ocean tastes like
Freedom.

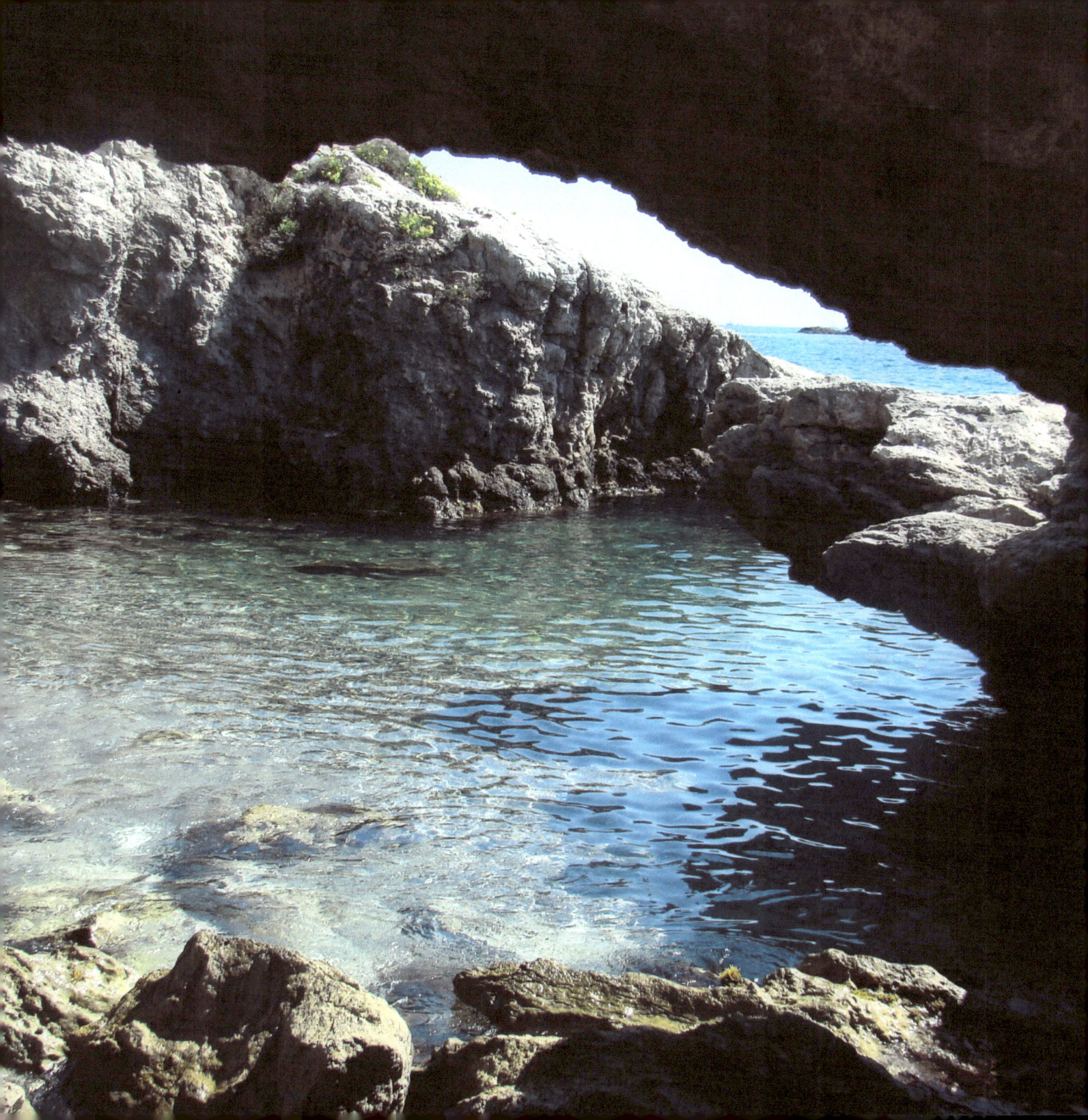

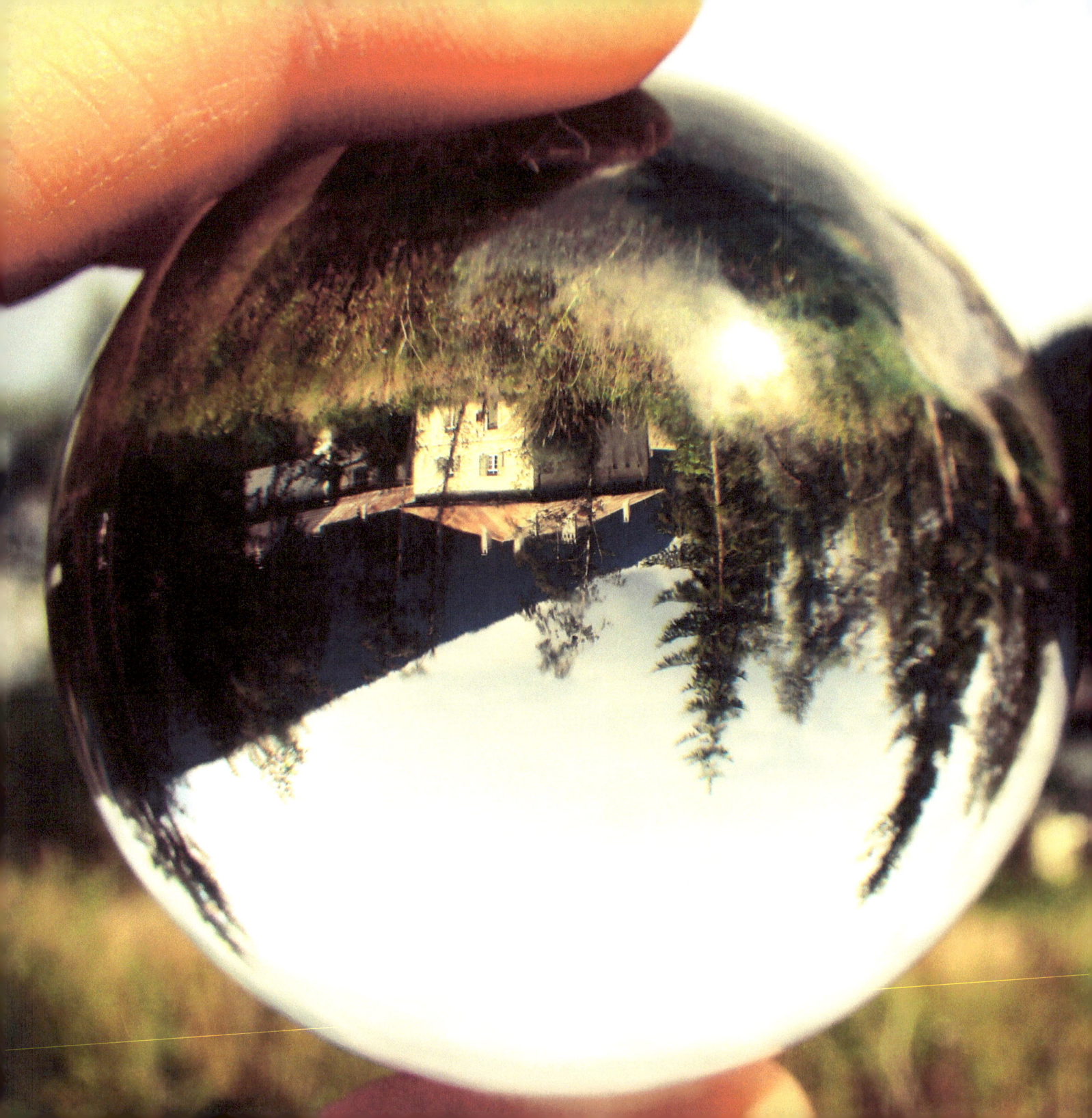

Slow down, take a break,
Open your eyes.
It will burn, you know,
It's the truth, you will see
Reality how it really is,
But it will hurt
Your eyes, make you
Cry, like the first time
You see the sun.
Not everyone is so strong
To keep the eyes open
And accept the truth,
The reality
Maybe try to make it better,
Fight
For the good things,
Which most of the people don't see,

Because most of them
Close their eyes again,
It's easier going back to
Your crystal ball
And stay there
Comfortably.
But what's the point?
What can be your mission
If you just do nothing?
How can you say you
Have lived
If you
Haven't explored,
Seen,
Grown,
Changed,
Made things better?

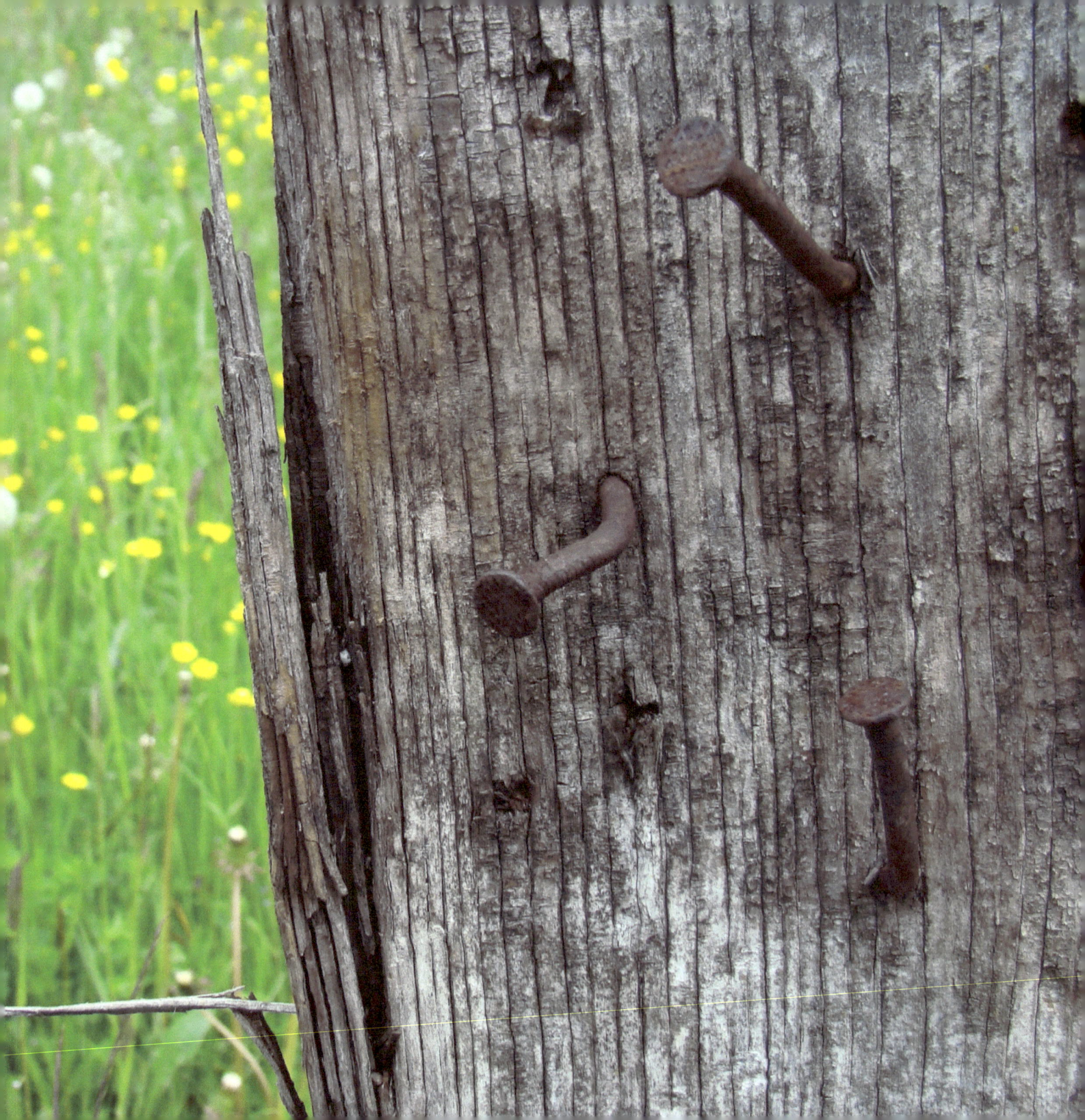

Feeling the bullet slowly
Entering my skin,
Burning what's around
But giving me a sense
Of peace and freedom.
Everything around me turns
Black
And the only thing I see is you.

The spider's last moment.

Those branches that aim at the sky,
Their green shines under the sunrays.
At some point everything,
With no life,
Collapses,
Falls down because of lethal hands.
Only this chair made of rings stays
In memory of the past seasons,
Like a book it treasures,
In whatever is left of it's body,
Stories of starry nights,
Heavy and snowy winters,
Perfumed summers.

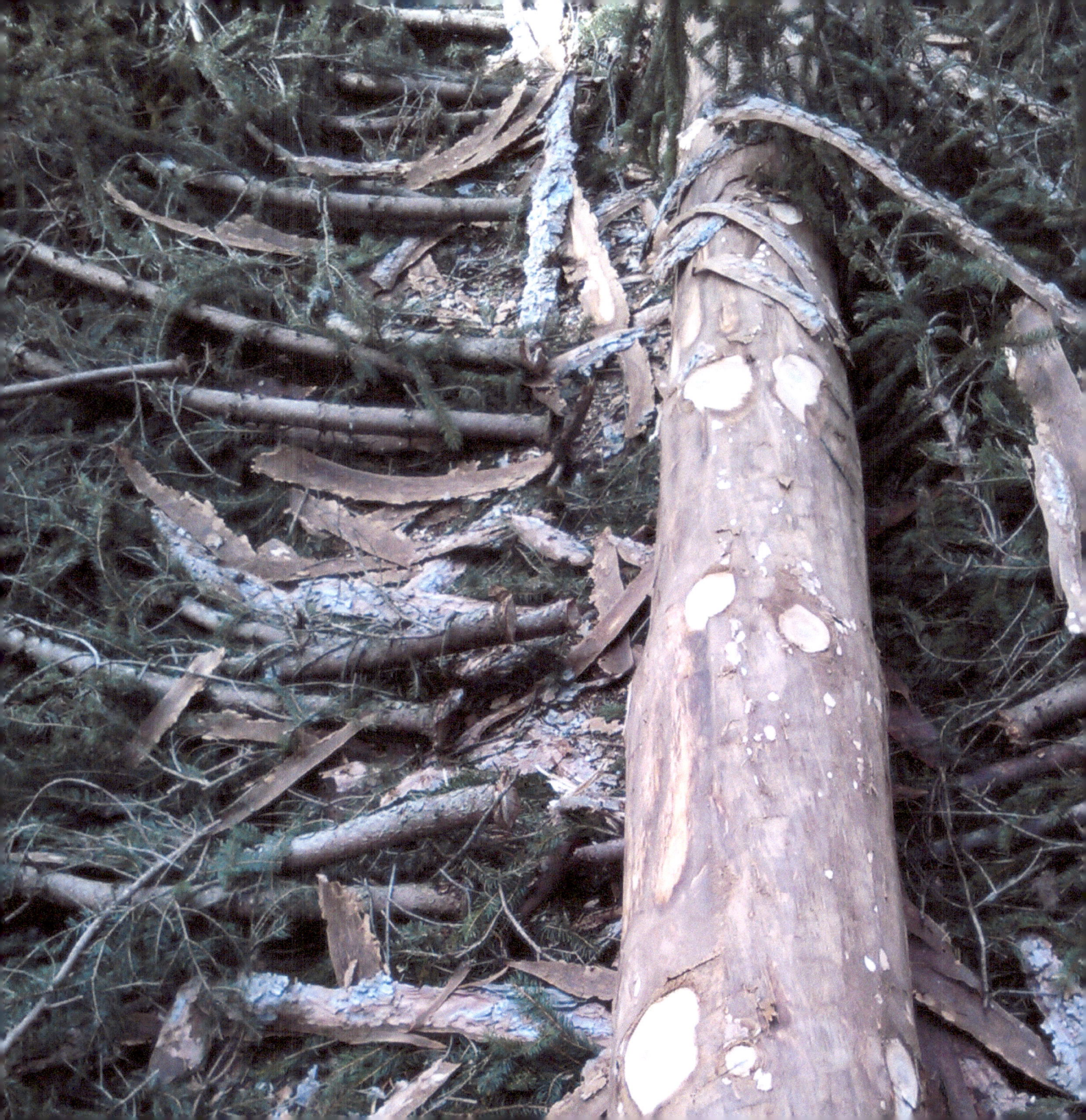

I see the truth through a
Kaleidoscope.
The world covered in water or
Smoke?
My tornado is resting,
My gypsy soul sleepy,
Relatively calm
Thinking deep
Surrounded by cotton stars.

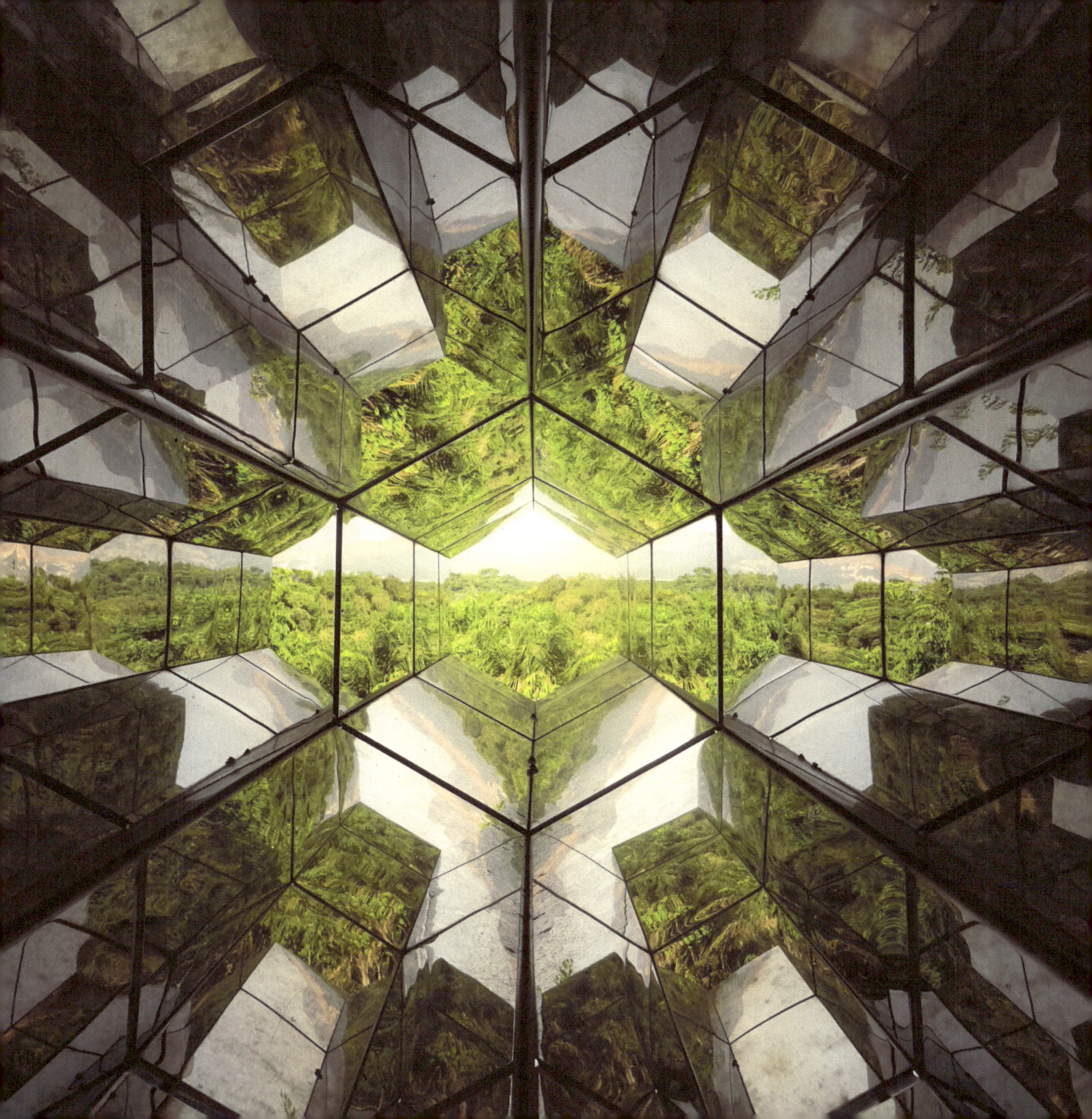

Walking in the sunshine
My eyes closed
The wind in my hair,
The heat on my skin,
A smile on my face;
Stranger in the place I grew up.
I don't belong here,
But I know I will find home.

How can I love all this,
But at the same time want to go away?
How can this be normal,
Having everything, but
Not wanting anything?

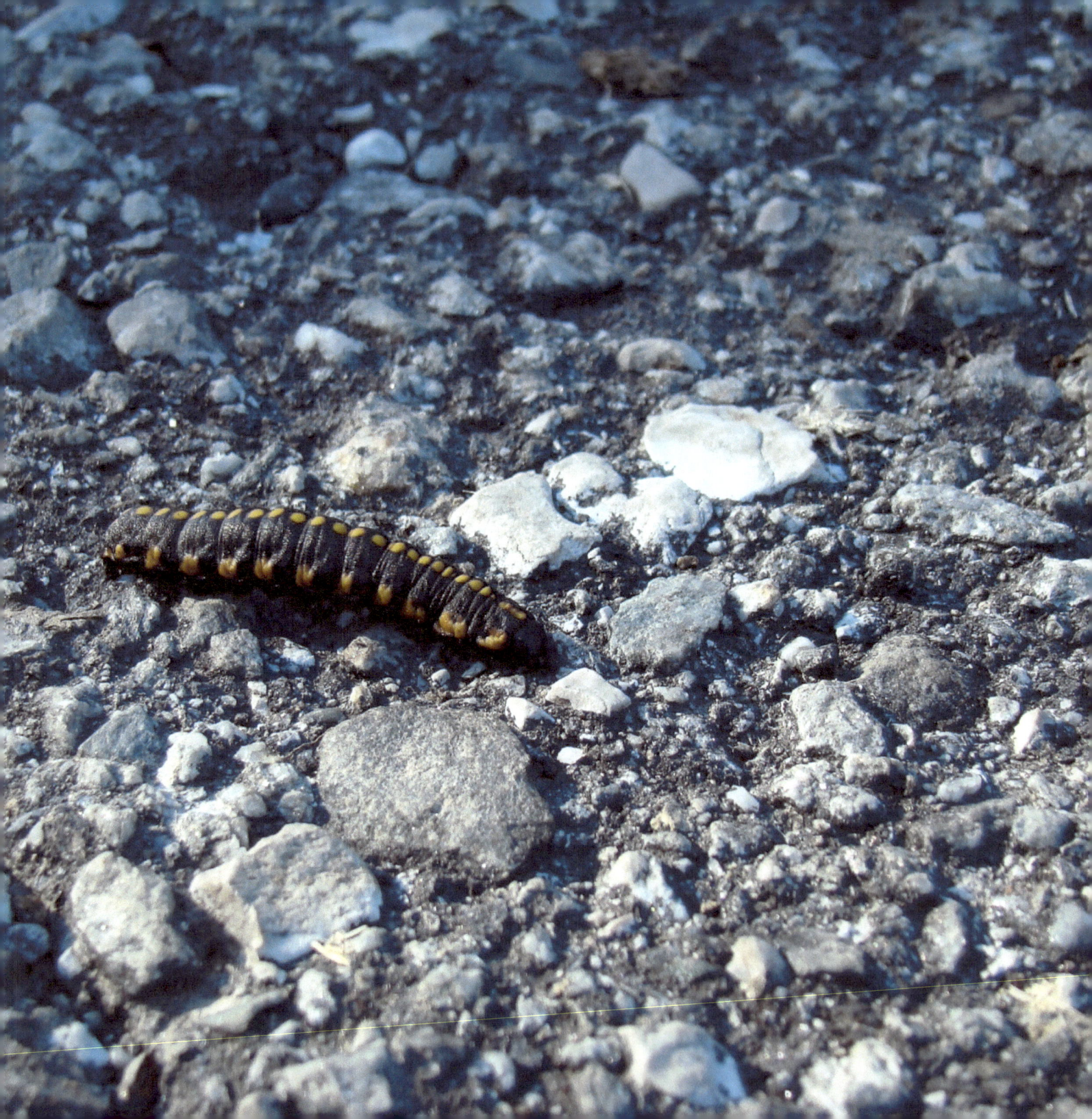

Feeling my feet blocked
In concrete
Heavy.
In a bubble made of
Superficiality, living in that
Reality makes me feel
Sick,
How can you spend all the time like
That?

Why do the thoughts turn up the volume at night?
Why do I feel incomplete if I exactly know what I want to do?
Maybe because I am still here, but
I will travel and see the world,
I will become one soul with the Earth
In different cultures and languages, colours and shades,
I will learn, understand,
Explore,
Grow and always improve.
My gypsy soul will become
A mosaic of experiences,
Unforgettable moments,
A book full of chapters,
Stories and adventures,
An album full of faces,
Smiles, amazing landscapes,
A box full of
Love
Happiness
Harmony.

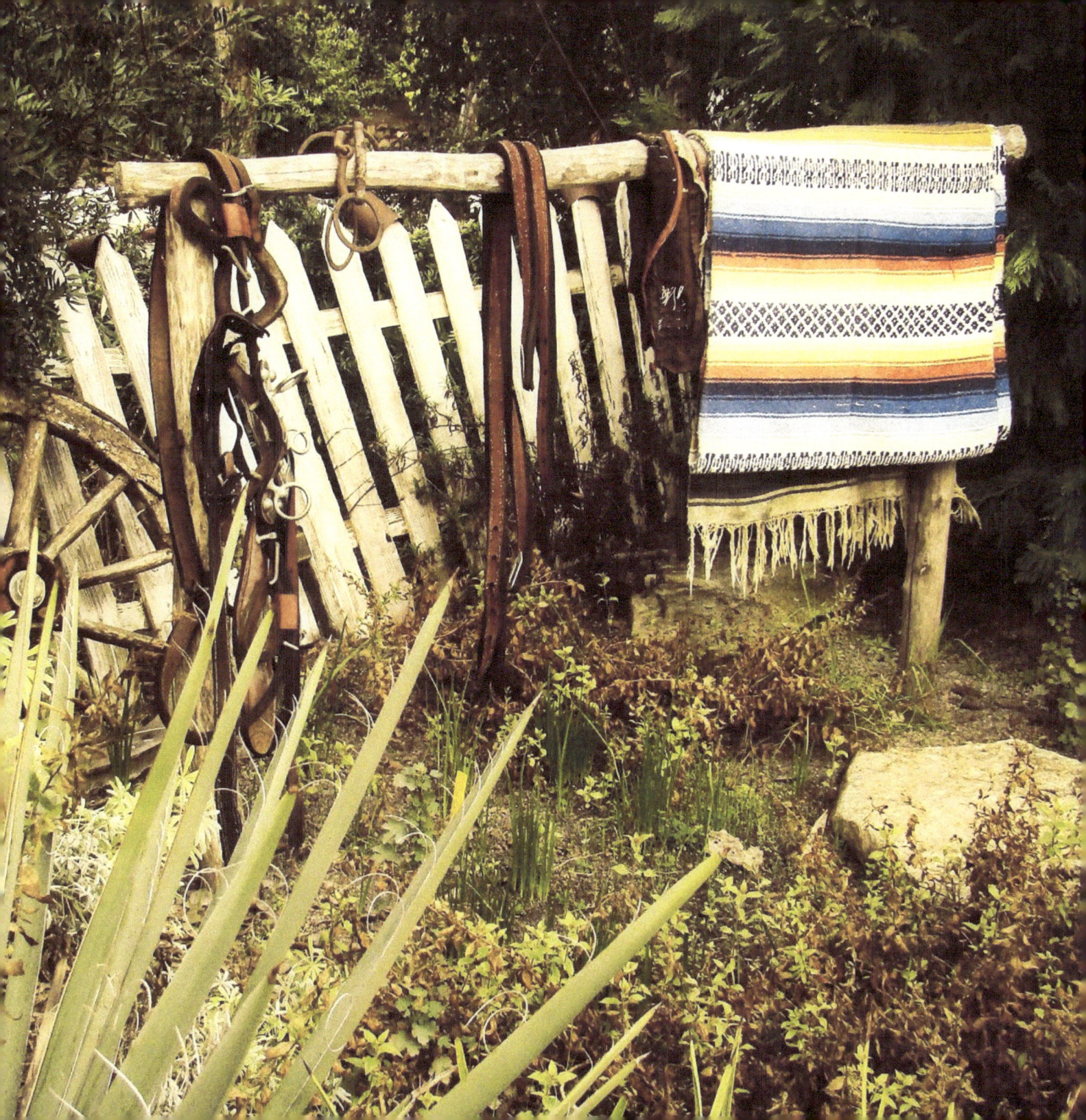

People are so blind.
Why can't they see the trees dance
At the song the wind plays?

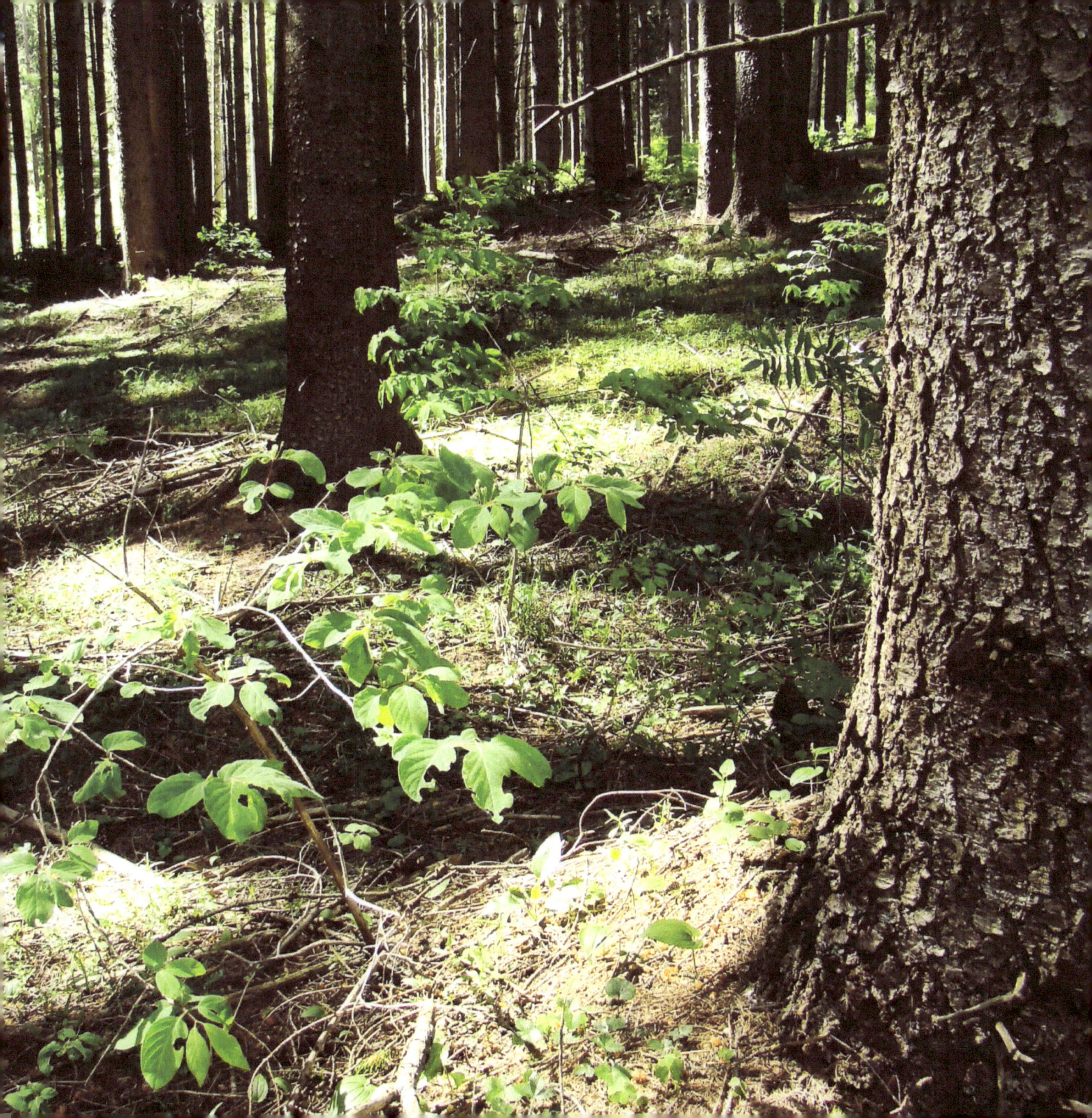

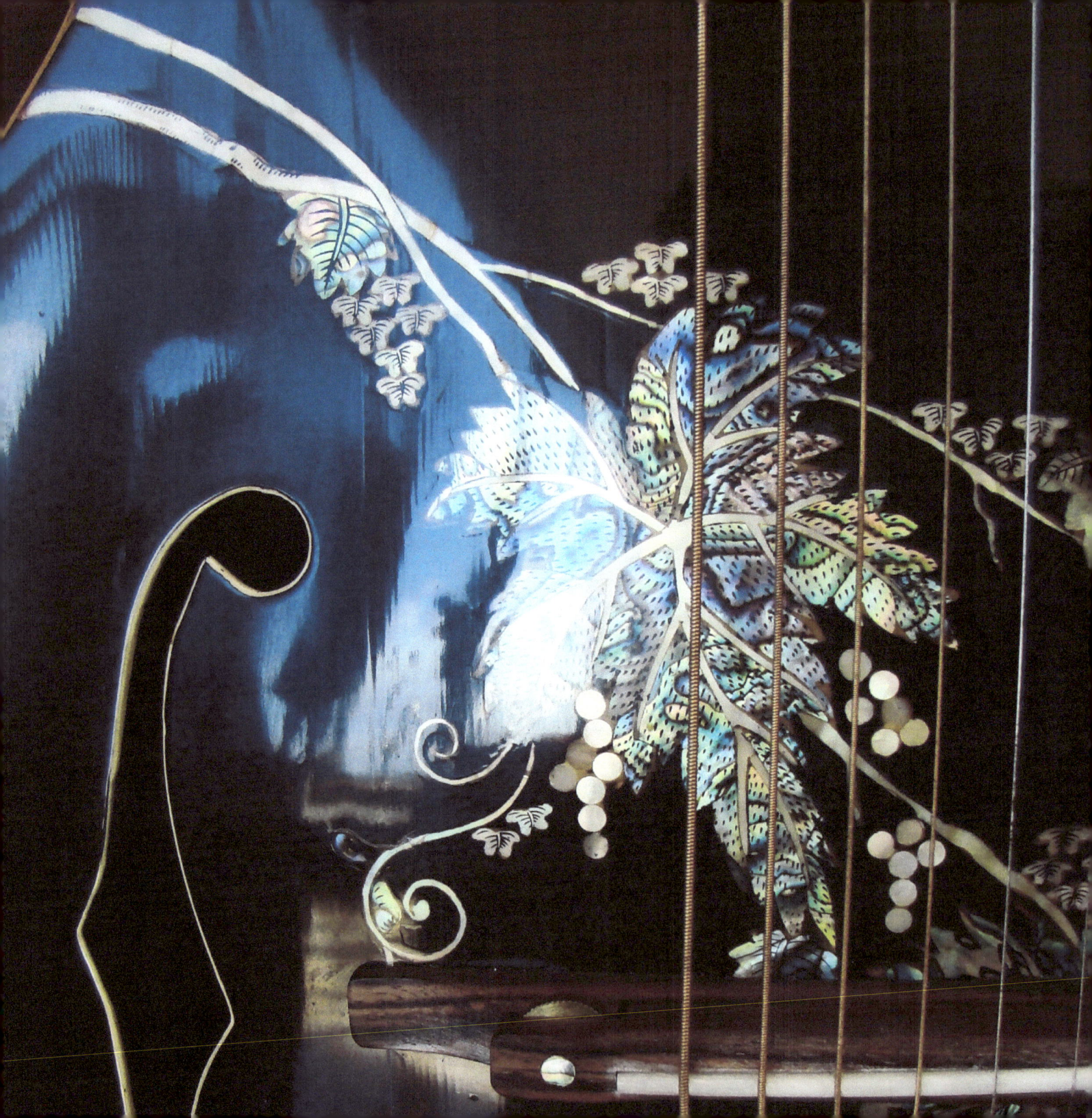

Stop being passive,
Live your life,
Squeeze it in your hands
And get the colours out of it,
Convert them into a indelible painting,
An artwork,
A song with shining notes,
A violin with golden strings
That will float over the waves
Of the water flowing
Through the wrinkles on your face.